OPEN SLOWLY

OPEN SLOWLY

Kate Light

Zoo Press

Zoo Press • P.O. Box 22990 • Lincoln, Nebraska 68542
Printed in the United States of America

Distributed to the trade by The University of Nebraska Press
Lincoln, Nebraska 68588 • www.nebraskapress.unl.edu

Cover Photograph: Maya Deren from her film *Meshes of the Afternoon*

Cover Design: Jason Schneiderman © 2003

Library of Congress Cataloging-in-Publication Data

Light, Kate
  Open slowly / Kate Light.-- 1st ed.
    p. cm.
  ISBN 1-932023-04-6 (alk. paper)
  1. Love poetry, American. I. Title.
  PS3562.I45392 O64 2003
  811'.54--dc21

                                                2002156146

zoo013

First Edition

Acknowledgments

The author gratefully acknowledges the publications in which the following poems appeared:

Barrow Street: "The Benefit of the Doubt"
The Carolina Quarterly: "Collecting Pretty Things"
The Dark Horse: "Greg's Legs" and "The Apple"
The Evansville Review: "Open Slowly"
The Formalist: "I Conclude a Sonnet" and "Phantom"
Gadfly: "Unknown Neighbor"
The Hudson Review: "On"
The Nebraska Review: "Man of Letters' Letter"
The Paris Review: "Reverence" and "Fate"
Pivot: "We Are," "Getting Serious," "The Brain," and "There Comes the Strangest Moment"
Rattapallax: "Courage," "Rules of Sleep," "There Are Others," and "Stoned"
Western Humanities Review: "At Interlochen"

Special thanks to the Bossak-Heilbron Foundation and the Corporation of Yaddo for their generosity and support during the completion of this manuscript.

Much gratitude to West Chester and Michael Peich for the amazing community; ever to Richard Howard, Dana Gioia, Molly Peacock, Robert McDowell, and Tim Murphy, for their leaps of faith.

Many have been very generous in the process: Bruce Adolphe, Cathy Ward McNally, Jerome Kitzke, Alison Woods, Rick Meier, Suzanne Noguere, Phillis Levin, Gerry Cambridge, Veronica Golos, Michael Milburn, John Aicher, Meg Campbell, Reinmar Seidler, Warren Stewart, Brandy Mow, Ram Devineni, Martin Mitchell, Jim Meddick, Marya Columbia, Ron Fletcher, Lois Finkel, Devorah Shubowitz, and Steve, Judy, and David Light; also Laurie Doti and Jan Cortner, so much help to my family. New thanks to newly-met Sarah Antine, Donna Masini, and William Pitt Root.

Also to Jason Schneiderman and Eric Kater, heartfelt thanks.

Table of Contents

Fall

Winter

Spring

To my parents, Dorothy and Martin.

...say, a square of stars
In the windowpane, suggesting the abstract
And large, or a sudden shift in position
That lets one body know the other's free to move
An inch away, and then a thousand miles,
And, after that, even intimacy
Is only another form of separation.

—Howard Moss, "Rules of Sleep"

Fall

Open Slowly;

someone may be standing on
the other side. Open slowly so you know
you're swinging wide
of them, and then
step through.

You may be you
once you are over being over-
wrought. See,
now,
how that was not
fair; it should not have been
so hard to get—to let be—
there.

Open softly,
and then shout
It's me!
once you are out.

Love guardedly, if you love;
do not push, or shove—
do you understand?

This will be your task,
not to command,
but ask.

Maybe Hidden

is my favorite space. Maybe finding
treasure buried underneath a mound
of brow, or cowering behind a binding
fear; tracing over and over the same ground
until some artifice gives way...Perhaps I'd rather
bring somebody out than be myself brought
out. That bit of him that I can gather
while the rest runs wild—I never doubt
its verity or value; but if one who's not
so reticent throws a rope my way, do I reach out?
Or retreat into some quiet place
where I can dream without intrusion
about my love, and how he loves seclusion...

Courage

Courage: not quite a cure or yet a curse—
instead a stage you reach, the Age
of Courage, your heel-digging getting even worse;
more insistently you're the one idiotic sage
rewriting theories, allowing no record
to be dire enough, no tendency so strong,
no cost so huge you can't afford
to risk it, no wait too hopeless or too long.
And you call it *courage*—to encourage
the un-ideal, indulge the self-indulgent,
to redesign the wheel. Then all the lectures
and the observations are for naught—
you go for low probabilities, conjectures,
against everything you have been taught...
And call it *Courage: neither curse nor cure*—
all for that one commodity that no one can insure.

Funny, As in a Man,

one man, for instance, trying
to express tenderness with no model to base
his take on it on. How this severe face
struggles to be concerned, to be clear; shying
just short of simply saying what
he wants to say (or does he not
know?). As in a poet explaining, *Class,*
if you know what you want to say, you
will be clear; and if you don't (sarcasm
here), *nothing will help you get through,*
not even a room full of anxious coaches.
Funny. As in this man, whom
it happens I feel quite tender towards,
stumbling on his attempts to put in words
kind words. Trying more direct approaches,
a drunken bull in a matador
shop, he's lurching at the spinning room;
searching, looking for a door,
to open into what—one can assume—
would be a wider field, a fuller range.
Look at him. It's kinda funny, I mean, strange.

Getting Serious

Sometimes you stumble into Getting Serious,
a cigarette dangling off of your lips.
How did you get there—were you delirious,
airborne, still up after one of your trips,
harvesting brain cells like a slick parasite?
Half-asleep did you sign something one night,
get drunk and marry some chick you'd just met?
How did you get there, how did you GET
SERIOUS, a fiddle thrust into your hand, lady
by your side? Shit. And now you're *calling* her, frantic
the night she's not home yet, swearing you don't care,
swearing that nothing's going on, *NOTHING, mind you,*
         ROMANTIC—
it's just that...you're *concerned*, because she's NOT THERE.
IS SHE ALL RIGHT? It's 2 AM, and you're sort of
her mother I mean her father now, her brother, more like;
it's caring, that's all, wondering, not *love;*
like what if she DOESN'T COME HOME, small as a pike
and you're a salmon left swimming upstream
in the rills of your own chiselled brain.
High as a kite. Stumbling into bed.
Tired as hell. Not-right in the head.
So what? It's good for the soul. When in Rome.
Hey there, I'm serious. When you coming home?

Choice

From any answer, twenty questions.
From every pathway, fifty escapes.
   (Did I say twenty? What of suggestions?
   Interpolations? Comments, japes?)

For any statement, untold responses.
For every poem, so many forms.
   (Endless parade of nonces,
   deviations from the norms.)

To every chamber, god, such pumping.
To any muscle—unfathomed nerves.
For every honest act, such trumping.
So much hurt out there, who here...deserves?

I cannot tell you why I feel certain,
In this chaos, only of you.
   (It's as if there were a curtain
   that keeps all others from my view.)

We Are

separated by a nightside table; you sleep
ardently, submerged in a translucent dream,
and I clear my throat periodically, deep
fogs of throat-gunk clogging me like cream
clogs an artery. Doesn't this seem
typical, your sleep clear sleep; mine troubled, neap
and low tides of it, with thoughts that creep
like crabs up a beach, progressing until the beam
or splash of wave comes to sweep
them back, crab-like thoughts that can't complete
a simple passage up the sunny beach...
I wish I could know what each
is inching toward, what path or street
a care fulfilled would lead my life to reach.
(You shift and mutter things, for thought and speech
are still like children playing hide-and-seek.)
Where now, my crustaceous thought-regime,
soldiers of the mind, bastions of advance-retreat-
advance? Still struggling with the moving sheen
of sun and sea: now one small room, now a dazzling gleam
of beach; now a sore throat to clear, secret-
ions of a weakened body-mind—and you, sweet
lambent sleeper, if you're some kind of promise-keep-
er, sing out to me, release, redeem.

The Brain

1.

"I saw a show about the body in the brain,
which they illustrated graphically,"
I tell you, *"cooked up a sort of visual chow mein,*
something for easy consumption, philosophically...
using what they call, I understand,
the 'video toaster.' Sometimes I've scoffed at the cartoon
ways by which a complicated idea gets hand-
ed down, but this was riveting: a blue balloon,
like a hot-water bottle with head and limbs,
wafted upward and backward, and wrapped
around the globe of the brain's upper rim,
lying back on it as one floating on water lies rapt
and sun-dazed..."
                        Blue water-bottle body, "self-
image"—a map collected on the mind's topmost shelf...

2.

One sleeps with this modelled self, its skills
burning in the brain; resting a hand that articulates and trills,
the elevation of the calves, an arm that plows
a canvas or a field. Skaters that slice
figure-eights, swimmers cutting through
the blue, the conductor handing out advice,
all those amazing things that people do...
The brain that moves and leaps and bounds
snuggles trimly, alertly, inside its crown;
while one that skips a bunch of rounds
in brain-body-land is always lying down,
or so I think, at bay in waitful laze
getting over a cold, for days, it seems, for days.

3.

Every day I wake up with another metaphor:
Self-Image, Self-Esteem, Ideal Self, or Self-Held-
Back. Erick Hawkins said: *Just before*
you dance, picture yourself dancing; then meld
with inner vision, let your new body be born.
But what of weight that won't stay lost, the sly
old body-in-the-brain refusing to be torn
from its mooring; illnesses clung to—"my" migraine, "my"
asthma, "my" hurt back?
       You have to be so deft
to let Self-Help help, and jealousy
play around you if it must; let someone be left
behind who always held you back, if need be.

4.

Now I don't want anybody else;
the body in my brain's already sleeping tucked
along the water-bottle of your belly.
Genetic, is it, this form? Ineluct-
able? How willingly the blueprint me
slipped a little to the side, so there'd be space.
In real life, it's more ungainly—
I sprawl, you sleep-talk; I watch your dreaming face
when I cannot dream, brain and body chasing
shadows, dodging disappointments lodged, say,
in an untoned hand, hand that should be phrasing,
foot that should be rising to a *relevé.*
Body that tries and tries to leap above
the rest, settle down, settle down, to sleep and love.

Greg's Legs

are long
strong
exhalations
of bone
and soft fur
draped all over
her;
unless
he is alone,
in which case
erase
all thought
of "draped"; they're not,
but laid
splayed
or folded to rest
in a nest
of down and cotton.
She's gotten
attached
to those thatched
legs
of Greg's,
no explanations,
confess-
ions or commentary
required
by *her*.

On the contrary.
She's never tired
of the extreme-
ly long fe-
mur,
and the thigh
rising high
to hook
into the nook
of pelvic socket.
And what of
her love
for the pocket
on the other end:
the bend
above
the clavicle
where the hollow dips
could store paper clips
in some radical
yet ancient
design?
Or her penchant
for the line of spine,
or running down the crown,
or going to town
on feeling
*every*thing

Rules of Sleep

With each of the men I've loved, a collection
not meant to be a collection, an unmatched set,
there has been some symbol of tender intersection—
in the sleep of us—that I thought I would not get
over, some resting of limb on limb, or sideward view;
but never one so lingering as this with you,
where the legs entwine to keep the body warm,
yours so long and softened by hair, and strong,
and completely let go on mine. A barber-pole form
flashes to mind, because we seem
entirely intertwined, and you travel as you dream.

Asleep, you speak in mutant tongues
I seek to interpret, and though you unconsciously supply
answers for my "What? What?", no matter how I try
I cannot catch the lyrics of your songs.
Rules of sleep where I'm concerned (and concerned
is a good word for it): *some cold seeps through.*
And not just chill to that hint of neck I've learned
to pull the errant comforter up onto—
but some future where no legs, at any rate, not yours,
entwine; some tragedy the tender night ignores.

Yours, Love, Is the Right Human Face

Life gives each of us a wheel of time,
I used to think, to roll along; no, not to roll—
to tread, to travel on; each a climb,
a continuum, a line, a corridor to stroll
at one's own pace; and in this way
we pass, or intersect, or take another's hand.

That's what I used to think when I was, say,
ten, or twelve, and to have a concept felt so *grand*.
How incredible (I thought back then),
that I can call Gareth on the phone
from *my* continuum, and *his* will let me in—
to pass like fish pass, intermixed, and still alone.
But that was long ago. I've changed, well, mostly,
gotten older, and known and loved more fish;
passed by them or been passed by, ghostly
waves lingering like some whispered wish
that hangs its blown-out breath behind in air.

Nine years' tendrils curl between
your lines of thought and mine. How clean,
to call it off for that.
                    How sensible.
                                How fair.

Winter

Attachment

Now I understand
   the wandering monk who knows
      attachment blows
         away like dust.
Now I understand to want, to lust,
   to watch the flickering needle: trust;
      to wonder where he is,
      with whom, to try hard not to assume,
is Attachment. And though I want to feel
   it's good—I'm told it's not.
  And with all the pain at play,
      I have to say,
         I must agree. To hurt is not
Good. *To love*, my friend Jerome
  says, *should be as natural*
      as breathing. Find me a home
like that, where love hovers
      in the air like breath.
   But to be lovers
      with one who does not love
        is...well, it is to live
        a living death.

Now I understand the sailor's wife,
   or astronaut's, whose life
      is tied in knots,
   who wants to set forth of her own
      accord, but can't—because
whenever she thinks that she can grasp
  the sense of things,
    just then, the clasp
      breaks free, her hands slip;

he has jumped ship,
    and Is is Was,
and asking why is like a crime.
    So who can climb? So who can climb,
        when the rope
        (invisible at best)
            which is looped around your chest,
                harboring your heart,
                    and which is your only hope,
                is frayed and torn apart.
Now I understand.

But He Carried

But he carried—I want to say,
he carried a blanket, oh, I don't know,
under his arm, or in a backpack, he carried
a blanket for us the whole way...
I want to tell my friends, to pull, harried,
on their arms, *Listen, he did;* he walked slowly
for my hurt back and carried things
wherever we went. He chose places, too,
that he wanted to show me, and pulled strings
to get me to go. He promised to help, to do
extra tasks to create time and space
so that I would say, *Yes, I will,*
and go with him somewhere, a place
he'd chosen, on a day he'd chosen. Shoved
things aside to make the time, and spill-
over time, more time, any time. He loved
to show up, call up, surprise me on the stairs;
and he carried things, carried me
up stairs and into rooms and never stopped
that kissing the whole time. *Where is he?*
Who is this man who stares at me with hate
in his eyes, chisels what is already cropped
to almost nothing, makes me wait
weeks before he gives the slightest nod?
Crushes, dispenses, dispenses with—this angry god?

Phantom

At the edge of consciousness it floats,
shimmering, phantom-pale and whole;
sentences, sometimes of words sometimes of notes—
lost ghost of youth or truth's jewelled ghoul—
visible from this distance that increases with each
moment of becoming increasingly awake.
We all have these inside, just outside of reach.
How I envy those who dream only for dreaming's sake,
or those whose lives are dream enough—
a little nightmare mixes into every breath I take,
and inventory takes me as I wake; not Love
will greet me with a smile, not help me bear
the burden of this, phantom more & more not there

ICU

When my father woke up, they asked him where he was.
The Purdue gymnasium, he said; not a bad guess
with all the noise and lights and action.

They asked if he knew why he was there; he said, *Yes*,
and carefully repeated back what he'd been told:
By-pass surgery. A small stroke. A fraction-

of-a-fraction of your world is all that's required
of you, to satisfy the huddle-round. You see?
To know your name, your children's names, your town—

perhaps profession, if it hasn't been too long...
This is to be the daily litany, the song
of brand-new, in a sense, innocence—*Are you tired?*

Are you in Pain? Do you need some water?
Would you like to watch TV?
We brought you a cassette player, a CD player, a CD—

Do you know why you're Here? Look who's here,
Sweetheart. Sweetie. Hon. Dear. Your daughter.
(He always hated to be called those things. Me too,

till now. Till I got scared. Or lost. Or old.)
Beep, beep. Beep beep beep beep.
The lights stay on all night. His feet are cold.
Are you tired? We'll let you sleep.

Pain Does That to You,

makes you test, and test, and test, and throw
things back in people's faces, things you know
you do not mean, and that they never dreamed
they'd hear from you, who once had only schemed
to make them feel their very best. *Oh floodgate*
fear that opens like a broken valve
and can't be stopped with sand or slate,
or sleight of hand, or words, or looks, or help, or salve.
Then when you see the pain that crosses
the threshhold of a loved one's face, or when
you know with every effort she embosses
and hides that look, to come back again
into the fray of you—what do you do?
Withhold, or give, admitting that what you knew,
you *knew;* & it was pain that spoke, not you?

At Least Three Nights

I.

At least three nights I have been sleepless.
This is nothing. Your body is a minefield.
Any moment it can explode—vein, heart, clot.
Who invented this? Who named it "stroke" as if naught
but a little caress? Who made you yield?
Who made us stand around here being helpless?

II.

He drew the Beautiful Hospital, which he missed.
The lawn, and the perfect pitch of parking lot.
We could not take him back there, nor did he insist.
It was not a case of *We love you, we love you not.*

I will never be at peace with this. Life is less
like its image and more like its husk.
His body is a skull. Every daytime is a dusk.
Forgive me for not being more transparent, more clear.
This whole thing has shaken me to the core.
Here—this is for you. And this.
And there's more. There's more. There's more.

Anemone

Half or more asleep my mind is writing
and my hand moves on a not-real page
a pencil it does not hold, inviting
words to incubate that never reached that stage.
What would those tendril words be weaving
into meaning if they had been had?
What would that page be holding salvaged, saving
something which of being might have been so glad?
Wait. Now you're saying notes you put onto a stave
have feelings of their own like joy at being?
I think that is the kind of thing born in a cave
of self bonded only to its own blind seeing.

There is a world out there that's real and gives
regardless of some poem that doesn't live or lives

At Interlochen

At Interlochen Arts Academy, a boarding high school for
the arts in rural Michigan, students are not allowed cars.

Graduation eve night, your father brought
    the car from Minnesota, and slept
in the campus union. That hot
graduation eve night, your father brought
your demons out—something not
    unfamiliar to me. Something surged and swept,
graduation eve night. Your father brought
    the car from Minnesota, and slept

unknowing. You took the astonished car and me
    and drove fast on the narrow highway
lane, drove fast until, *suddenly*
knowing, you took the astonished car and me
onto the shoulder—and in pitch black we
    sat, waiting, till your dark clouds went away.
Then you took the astonished car and me
    and drove fast on the narrow highway

back, silenced. Only later I thought
    we could have been killed, and wept.
Was that what you wanted? To be caught,
silenced? Only later I thought
    over how little I had tried to intercept,
or break into your garrotted
silence. Only later I thought,
    we could have been killed, and wept.

Man of Letters' Letter

His last letter to me. With the same-as-ever
tiny script, so small the pencil'd barely waver
as he wrote—and toward the end—or all along?
he didn't watch his hand, but wrote by rote, beyond
the beyond. And because he could not see the left
side of the page, halfway down he'd start to drift
at first to drift to the right and to let his writing
shift as well—a train of thought so trained that fighting
illness and despair did not forfend its intelligence
Who is the Canadian there at Yaddo, I wonder; and the
Irishman? Could it be Alice Munro? If so,
you are with the best. Cynthia
says of her, "She is our Chekhov.
And the one from Ireland will be the great
successor to Frank O'Connor—Is he
William Trevor? How I admire them!"
and then he'd tell a hellish tale
I pray was just a dream of how a male
nurse came into his room and
threatened him for disturbing
him and then the
margin grew narrow
er and narrow
er until only
one or two
words fit
into the
space as
if there
were a
great
funnel or
kind of
a brain
or spine
breathing
down
the
world
into
its
stem
and
then
he
was
sign-
ing
off
with
so
much
love

On

Strange, that the world goes on
(a stranger's screaming in the street)
Strange: that you who were here are gone
and we here, we weep and we sleep and we eat

I won't pass again through a door
of a room on a sterilized hall
I won't climb the stairs to a third or fourth floor
with your name on a plaque on the wall

outside; smile and call to you—*Hi,
it's Kate*—and see you turn—which is hard—
And if I'm late, then, to start saying why...
You're smiling at me; there's the reward

for the travel, and all of the work of getting
there

Spring

I Never Want to Go When It's Time

I never want to go when it's time
to go; I want to hang back, to read
a book, or make another line rhyme.
I always think that what I really need
is there in the place that I am leaving,
not waiting in the new place I ached
to go to. I go, but with a kind of grieving,
saying, *Why'd I ever wish to shake*
things up, when things were really fine?
To be with him I had to yank
my roots, I had to pull my bones
by heartstrings, to tear my spine
from land to land; sometimes I walked a plank
to reach that world, and breathe, and write these poems.

Here Lies My Heart

Here lies my heart.
It is as simple as
that. It leads me, in art
and life; it is
that simple. It's making a pass
at you, an extended
play (a year-by-year
affair, all schiz-
ophrenic bliss
and disrespair.)
I befriended, tried to,
anyway, Despair, and his
faithful if misguided
sidekick, Hope.
In fact, *you* introduced us!
So if you see me go
arm in arm with these two
gentlemen,
well, don't get too excited.

Here lies me,
a Chinese box:
inside, a drawer,
another drawer.
(Behind a face another
face my father, my mother,
for instance.) Here
the innards of a few
spilled out, right out
here in full view.
What will you do?
Or more to the point,

what *did* you do?
And I with you?
The contents, thrown
every which way,
all discontents; you say
you can never have it put
back away.
If I had only known.

Here lies *your* heart,
more to the point.
I've gladly set
my own aside
to put things right.

When in Ellipses

When in ellipses of unequal passion
two bodies orbit (and often, Love, they do),
the one who moves in more the tumbling fashion
(head over heels is awkward, I think, don't you?)
is transparently helpless; the wind whips caution
from her grasp, sears her hair, streaks through
her resolve. One glimpse of him's intoxication;
while (these are mere samples here, these two—
she and he could have the roles reversed,
or by two of the same sex be replaced),
with her love an atmosphere supporting
him, he enjoys a blissful soar through space.
We could name one Lucky and call one Cursed.
(Unless this painful love's rewarding?)

Whale Bone Pelvis Moon

Whale bone,
pelvis moon,
pale bowl—

I crave you whole.

Poor soul.

We debate about
a spiritual state.

Devout,
at your bone-body,
I worship the one great act;
a pact
to love
another
before dying out.

You,
so much in doubt,
refuse to consecrate
the thought.
*That's not
spiritual!* you shout.

Please don't shout.

(We don't see
eye to eye,
needless to say.)

Keep love and sex separate, you cry,
in this place, anyway!
and close our case.

Thanks a lot.
My god,
I've prayed,
outside, in rain,
for your safe
return to my house—

And not in vain,
for here you are;
the crest
of your hip
against my breast.

But you will not concede,
will not convert,
will not bow to need
or admit hurt.

Oh no; you just protest, and such,
skeptical,
iconoclastic: *Too much*,

while this ideal
of mine, this idol, *feeling*
(plastic, cryptic,
yet in the final analysis,
revealing),

crumbles to dust.
You call it lust.
I aim above.

I'll worship here
at the curve
of your hip—

and have the nerve
to call it love.

The Benefit of the Doubt

Just might be that the doubt doesn't benefit
me any longer; was more a habit than a tool
to get through meaner times. In and of it-
self, the concept of the Doubt is cool—
it holds one back from drawing the worst
conclusions; for there are corners you can't
look round, things you haven't thought of at first
glance, a world beyond the mantle
of circumstance one hasn't seen behind.
It lowers the blood pressure (there's a nice
benefit), and wakes a different piece of mind
than the one that refuses to think twice,
but jumps first to its conclusion, then to its demise,
shot through with confusion, and wiser in no wise.

I Know What the Answer Is—

I know what the answer is—it isn't fame
or fierceness, the ability to argue down to ash
another's flaming tree; to be a household god or household name
(though this is nice), to make the biggest splash
when landing in the oceans of...the tides of the affairs
of men and women; good lord, no, no, not cash;
not forty messages on the machine—who cares
(unless, of course, you care about the people who
are leaving them), oops—I almost let it slip;
I came *that* close—a little clue.
What the answer is, at evening, what unsinking ship
I'm reaching for and clinging to;
I have always, always, always known.
Am I alone in this? Am I alone?

Neglected Plant

Neglected plant, it fed upon itself and air
as long as it was able.
It leaned to the left, and, waiting there,
became the basis of a fable.

The plant not fed or watered is
the model of our affair;
the analogy's mine, the concept his—
the plant that feeds on air.

Remember

when you're lonely in your room, and the year
is hovering in your eyes; remember, when
he calls you late and sorry, how the tears
had made you wise; how it happened again
and again, pushing you out and pulling you in,
and how his words were wind that fanned your fears;
how he could not help himself, though his skin
was sweet and soft, and though—when you were near—
he was drawn to you; how his body was truth and on-
ly his body was truth—no, no, remember how lost
you felt and how often, and how high the cost,
and how close Love sat next to Lone.
Remember—a whispering in your vein—how keen
the pleasure, but how stabbing deep the pain.

Stoned

He came to her door drunk and stoned,
and glaring with slant-eyes of hate.
He made her feel ravaged, dethroned;

but she kissed him. He staggered and moaned
and could not support his own weight.
He swayed at her door drunk and stoned,

leaner and lankier-boned,
and reeking of cigarettes. Great.
He also looked ravaged, dethroned,

full of sadness. Madness. She zoned
an ear to his lips. "Smells like Kate,"
he said. "You're drunk and you're stoned—

I *am* Kate!" And he said, "I know."
That is how things escalate.
He makes her feel ravaged, dethroned.

They should have been chaperoned.
Now she's bereft. *Separate.*
He came to her door drunk and stoned;
and left her there ravaged, dethroned.

Summer

I'll Be Right Back

and left front, and left back and right
front. I'll be the back you back off from,
the light you seal the crack
against, what you cannot numb
yourself to, never could. I'll tell your story,
if I must; I'll *be* a kind of must
that settles on the inventory
of your bones, your tendrils, and your trust...
I'll come—because I can't by day—by night,
and find the heart nestled into
your silken chest, and kiss
the perfect curving ribs that I so knew;
and you will stir, and whisper, *who is this?*
And you will dream of being back beside
the back you eyed and eyed and eyed.

If He Sees Her

If he sees her, love will flare
briefly; a struck match, held
in his fingers, that he will let
burn till the threshold of flesh is threat-
ened. It will burn, and he will stare—

the meeting of the sulphur and the air—
and the dark will be dispelled
briefly. Briefly he will forget
his anger, briefly light be
led into his darksomewhere

soul or self or heart or cleft or bare
closet. But say he burns and he will deny it;
say he loves and he'll mortify it.

The Body, Without

The body, without the touch it cannot live
without, lives. *The body that can't unwrap*
for any other body steps into a trap
of its own making. The heart that would not give
has found a way not to have
to give. *The mind that stands accused*
can't let its phantom fists relax.
The mind that thinks the very worst of love
can think its worst in peace. *Unused*
to peace, in silences it dreams attacks.
                                            Save
these pilgrims, set them back on truth's true course.

Through this maze, there must be swaths
to cut, short cuts or long. Pace hope's floors
and breathe perfumes locked inside of doors;
batter them down with persistent shoves,
these doors that have been shut for years.
Heal the bitter with the touch of tears.
Give the body back the body that it loves.

Another Show About the Brain

...this time, to explain about addiction—
and the formation of the adolescent
brain: how, during that time, it's about connection
and rewiring, refiring—incalescent
and competitive—the survival of what's fit,
what fits, and what's already in use.
(So, say, musical lines that one can commit
to memory, may remain and reproduce—
but those math problems, problematic and obtuse,
can get tossed forever from the garden.
One example that I thought of, watching.
Tools to get babes, tools to *be* babes—pardon
the un-P.C.-ness of me—catch-phrases are so catching.)

The brain is a jungle gym, a playground,
a hotbed if you will, absorbing and releasing,
party in the head, mixing its own clay, ground
being broken, uncovering, discovering, increasing.
You get the idea. And dopomine, key-turner,
messenger, carrier pigeon, essential
acid, what-have-you, the agent and the learner,
the test tube and the burner,
ping-pongs onto the scene, plays tag with dendrites—potential
and eagerness. OK. So say you've got cocaine
or another substance, raising pleasure levels till the brain
outpeaks its peak experience (orgasm) to top
the top—Now you're hooked. And cannot stop.

And *then*—here's the rub, there had to be
one—everything else looks pale, tastes bland, feels
dull; bit by bit the pleasure of one's life peels
away. And—this is the part that really had me—
it doesn't have to be a drug that does it to one.
It could be a...something else—that courses through one...
And then it gets to be: *where's the next high
coming from?* alternating with emptiness and the wish to die.
I love these shows about the brain. They give you 'you'
whatever way one goes about it, since you've got one too.

A Blip on the Radar Screen

is how a friend of the woman he left me for
described it. "Oh, he was nothing to her," she said,
and then I stared at her, not really, more
internally, I stared in shock; in the red
reaches of my temperament began a beeping,
as when a truck backs up. He just had
her a while, but what everyone ignored
was me, me in an emergency state,
blood gushing from my core,
for two months, or more,
while they were making love and sleeping.
Surely I have stumbled through a gate
into another world, where people's brains
have been removed and drained, and filled with slate
or cement or sand and then set
free, to get whatever they can get.

There Are Others

There are others whom I miss, yearned toward
in this breathing world, friends whose faces
turned, whose looks explained what a word
meant to them, took me to their hearts, places
I miss. We are still here but we're slipping
from each other every day, even as we come
in close, wrapping our souls even as we are stripping
them bare. Oh beloveds, is there somewhere
to go where no one wants what another
cannot give, no one has come to care
too little or too much, no one sees as a brother
one who wants to be a lover; and no one sits
tear-blind by the door or by the silent phone,
their heart breaking into a thousand little bits,
feeling deeply, finally, irretrievably alone.

The Apple

I know what you are like with another woman,
because I know what I was like with another man:
how there is a screen inside where a movie plays,
where a hopeful self has an upturned face;
while a new wish to respond stirs to a come-on
which may be innocent or part of a plan
to push someone out of the way & into the haze
of oblivion, you-hurt-me-look-how-I-can-hurt-too—
(was this *me?* was this *you?*) and how you *recall,*
how memory calls out to you, louder & louder the closer
you get to the edge of letting everything go—
like all the photos about to be dumped into a river,
a packet of letters burned into ash, sensations
killed off with a jagged knife and all locations
denounced. How you think that you will never forgive,
never; better to *forget* things too numerous to mention,
whatever was so necessary once.

Also I've felt it rise in me, like a serpent, a terrible
earthquake, a selfish, devouring flood—-
to tell it seems the only bearable
choice—how there is a vengeance so out for blood.
I know what you are like with her, how you bend
over her breasts, how she laughs aloud
over her prize, your long body and beautiful hands
that can cover so much with one proud
reach, how your eyes get big as desire sweeps
through them. That was why I could not keep
away no matter what terrible thing I deeply knew,
about how love dies in a certain broken valve in you—
I know how it is, my love, for I have done it too...

Fall

Load Up

Load up, some spirit whispered in my ears,
some fairy pricked my arm when I was spawned.
You'll need to carry things around for years.

You'll be a packanimal with two careers.
There will be much of which you're overfond.
Load up, the spirit whispered in my ears.

Too bad you won't consort with gondoliers
who'll take your goods aside and glide them swanned,
and carry them around for you for years.

Enough stuff to fill up hemispheres.
You'll be a sort of rooted vagabond.
Load up, the spirit whispers in my ears.

Papers, recordings, souvenirs—
assorted, hoarded; you'll be in junk bond-
age to things you've carried 'round for years.

May as well enjoy it. Cheers?
It's the *feelings* that exhaust. *Relive, respond,*
load up, some spirit whispers in my ears.
You'll need to carry this around for years.

Collecting Pretty Things,

which I thought, at first, would be a phase
I passed into and out of (after the monk phase
when all I wore was brown and every place
I walked I stopped to touch the soft faces
of flowers), became a desire not to erase
but to concentrate; mixing pinks and blues into my grays
and blacks, reaching out to dangling sparkly
baubled things for sale on velvet trays,
splashing color into hair hitherto hanging darkly.
Thrown back to my sixties childhood, I wrapped
a band around my forehead, selected
the brightest earrings, keen to be untrapped
from all that brown. So many small collected
things!—scarves and leggings, beads and shoes
that glittered, an embroidered bag—
all that, in some gypsy dream, I'd use
poised for a perfomance, photoed for a mag-
azine. I'd been to Italy
and seen how they do it, put the stripes and plaid
and prints together on one single body,
and how somehow it never turned out looking bad
or weird, or overdone, or gaudy.
That was the beginning of entering giddily
into an experimental time, a grace
period—not too young, nor yet too old, for praise,
for eyes turning to follow me a little ways,
once caught by something uncommonplace
wrapping round, or hanging down, or falling open—
jacket, earring, fishnet stocking; some signal to give chase
I suppose—it was my pleasure phase, my pleasure phase.

The Lighter Side

I could feel how, when some chemistry
ran dry, it was like a curtain fallen down.
But when it would rise again, I could see
it in his face; I could see the lifting cloud,
origin of a smile so deep within
it was a wisp floating up at first,
a tiny shiver, and his eyes begin-
ning to...lighten. An eyebrow rising, an erst-
wildness, hint, whisper; at last, a true grin,
a flirtatious glance. What metaphor
is this: the lighting of a cigarette or candle?
Sunrise, stunning to me, all the more
a prize, kindling fire too hot to handle.
I lit him, and he lit me. Who lights
him now? and who burns, when he ignites?

Reverence

My body is so much bigger, and I am always wanting
to write a memoir. *The bow at the end of class*
is called a "reverence." Things keep waking me, haunting
my sleep. *After acknowledging the teacher, we may pass*
from the room, I am amazed to have reached this stage.
first giving, perhaps, a smattering of applause; then
Has my face caught up with, surpassed, my age?
rushing to the changing-room, to turn again
into little girls, My body is fuller, and seeks repose.
taking the spiked hairpins from their places,
Sleeping and waking are two sisters, pulling up close;
and striking the pleasant attitudes from our faces,
with their arms around each other, smiling for
the camera; *chattering of boys and clothes and school*
dances. even though inside me rages rage and war.
Time is exerting itself with a force more full,
a gravity more grave *We are hungry and thirsty and have*
than I could have ever imagined. Am I old
all the time in the world to learn to move
suddenly? Have I passed from the arena, the bold
spotlight, the field *as gracefully as any young swan.*
of all possibility? Is it time to bow graciously and pull
aside? To admire the young, till they also move on?

Little Miss

The child bled from me
before I knew I had
the child; which meant, you see,
no agonizing decision,
no sleepless going wild,
no invasion or incision,
no giving up the child.

When I gave the news I thought
I'd get something of you in kind-
ness. I thought, perhaps, some mad
rush of the mind
over to my side.   Not.

I didn't want to live and learn
this: you really could care
less. Had no sense at all
of wanting to be There.
Couldn't imagine in the least small

part what one was going through...
so even if one said that one was *fine*,
who could be so and be fine? Who?

Who could give four, five weeks a flood
of child-material and blood
and be fine? And who could turn
away from such a one? I learn
someone *could* turn away: You.

Things Have Gotten More Complex,

or else I'm trying hard to be more fair,
describing how I saw things, or what I think
may have happened; putting it out to air,
airing it, setting it, letting the ink

dry (as one ultimately has
to do—). It's gotten tougher than it was,
to say *this is what I think was true*—
and so I don't; I don't, because

the brain reconstructs the puzzle, builds it anew
every time it thinks the puzzle through.
He'll never believe it if I say I care
how he feels about the portraits there

in that gallery that poems become, I dare-
say; and I don't mean to be flip or debonair
or arrogant—which I guess will just add
another thing to the list of what he won't

believe. Ironic, isn't it, when people who
one doesn't know come in to take a peek—
but he, whom I adored, and still, admittedly, do—
will not condescend to call, or look, or hear, or speak.

Ironic—nothing! What it really is is sad
sadder saddest, the kind of thing to burn
and burn with no tomorrow and no return...

Practice

This practice, this habit of abandonment,
the reaction and the melting-down;
though no one should have to endure it,

if you are among the few who choose to drown
while your lover watches on the shore
and reaches out his hand, then you'll be sure
to understand.

         And you will know perhaps the path
of going back to the sources of the crime—
a rest, a sigh, a prayer, perhaps a bath—
and then letting the thing occur another time.

Unknown Neighbor

Hi, she says, leaning on the railing.
What are you doing, homework?
Well, sort of, I say. I'm waiting for my friend.
I'm waiting for my heart, she says.
(Me too, I think; my *friend*.)
Out on a long walk? I ask.
Well, she says, I have a girl friend, I've known
her 50 years; once in a while we get together
for dinner. She comes around here to Chelsea, she says.
Use to be I just had arthritis and rheumatism, now—it's a pain
in the neck—I got a convulsive heart. I come from
Twenty-second and Eighth, where I'm helping
my brother. For me that's a long walk.
So I wait.
I used to climb mountains! she says.
I was young like you, she says.
But I got no squawk—I've done a lot—
and maybe more to do, she says;
who knows? And, waving, off she goes.

Fate

Who can embrace the body of his fate?
—Roethke

But I embraced the body of my fate,
the body I sought to seal my body to;
one I would care for till the last great
moment of being me or being you.

I kissed and heard the whispered dreams,
body I dared to seal my body to.
Desire beyond, human-imal it seems,
that whispered body-being, You.

Pulled by heart to body, heart to touch,
the friend I thought my love my love was due.
Weeping, speaking too little and too much,
not knowing why it is anguish being you.

I have hurt this body; oh my fate
is sealed: that I must wrench my body to.
Promise, promise always but too late.
Fated is too fearful, being you.

Driven

Driven by anger buried deep inside
but crouching to erupt, like a geyser set
on a two-month timer; cocktail of hurt

and hurtful, neglected and neglecting, animal pride
and territorial blindness, crouched for a defensive spurt
or an offensive strike; all this, yet

wanting to be loved, to make love, to instigate
and respond, bend to a tender touch
or fierce, be gotten through to or to pierce; passionate

and I suppose afraid (this last used so much
as a kind of catch-all escape from the responsibility
of having caused anybody any pain); *this is he,*

I try to explain; why I stayed—why I cried
on the sidelines then went back in; sighed,
regrouped, tried again—failed—failed miserably,

and in a misguided attempt to get free, lied—
heard his voice—repented—repeated a mantra—*I love him so;*
could not, in any ultimate sense, till I was forced to, go;

relented, gave in to it, cave of desire and disarray—
wherein, if I could be, I would be, still, today.

There Comes the Strangest Moment

There comes the strangest moment in your life,
when everything you thought before breaks free—
what you relied upon, as ground-rule and as rite
looks upside down from how it used to be.

Skin's gone pale, your brain is shedding cells;
you question every tenet you set down;
obedient thoughts have turned to infidels
and every verb desires to be a noun.

I want—my want. I love—my love. I'll stay
with you. I thought transitions were the best,
but I want what's here to never go away.
I'll make my peace, my bed, and kiss this breast...

Your heart's in retrograde. You simply have no choice.
Things people told you turn out to be true.
You have to hold that body, hear that voice.
You'd have sworn no one knew you more than you.

How many people thought you'd never change?
But here you have. It's beautiful. It's strange.

I Conclude a Sonnet Never Changed

I conclude a sonnet never changed
a mind, or moved a heart, or opened a locked
door. If such could be so readily arranged,
poems could not possibly stay stocked.
Pockets would be filled and pillows swarmed.
Oh no, a sonnet never swung a gate,
cracked a safe, or left a bomb disarmed.
It never swam a moat, or pried a crate.
Or rather, whom it moved, at any rate,
was accidental; a side effect, some poor
someone tugged at when its influence, its weight,
its pool of moonlight revealed a midnight shore.
Yes, then, it may have changed a life, or more;
but not the one it was *intended* for.

Just the longing of any lover, the ache
for the beloved at any lover's core;
just any anger vanishing when I wake
and all I want's in you, more
than ever, more than I ever
hoped, though I hoped, through all
my ages—young and small, foolish, clever,
saddled into life or free to fall.
Just the loops, the secrets that we know
and why we do; so if a word is hard
or a day cruel, the turning will go
on, till the soul calls off its guard
and the wish that all of us were born into
rises up, and I come back, in joy, to you.